D0506172

Mary Queen of Scots

MA=   RIA.

Regina   *Scotia.*

Barbara Mure Rasmusen

First published in Great Britain by Heinemann Library
Halley Court, Jordan Hill, Oxford OX2 8EJ
a division of Reed Educational and Professional Publishing Ltd

OXFORD FLORENCE PRAGUE MADRID ATHENS
MELBOURNE AUCKLAND KUALA LUMPUR SINGAPORE TOKYO
IBADAN NAIROBI KAMPALA JOHANNESBURG GABORONE
PORTSMOUTH NH (USA) CHICAGO MEXICO CITY SAO PAULO

© Reed Educational and Professional Publishing Ltd 1996

All rights reserved. No part of this publication may be reproduced, stored in a retrieval system, or transmitted in any form or by any means, electronic, mechanical, photocopying, recording, or otherwise without either the prior written permission of the Publishers or a licence permitting restricted copying in the United Kingdom issued by the Copyright Licensing Agency Ltd, 90 Tottenham Court Road, London W1P 9HE

Printed in China

00 99 98 97 96
10 9 8 7 6 5 4 3 2 1

ISBN 0 431 07870 X

(Library stamp): Rasmusen, Barbar... Mary Queen of Scots / Barbara Mure Rasmusen JB MAR 1210096

British Library Cataloguing in Publication Data
Rasmusen, Barbara
Mary Queen of Scots. – (Scottish history topics)
1. Mary, Queen of Scots, 1542–1587 – Juvenile literature
2. Queens – Scotland – Biography – Juvenile literature
3. Scotland – History – Juvenile literature
I. Title
941.1'05'092

Acknowledgements
The Publishers would like to thank the following for permission to reproduce photographs:
Duke of Atholl: p.13 bottom; Blairs College Museum Trust: p.16 bottom, p.21; Bridgeman Art Library: p.8 top; British Museum: p.4 top, p.11 bottom right, p.12 right, p.17 top, p.18 centre; Collections Viollet: p.6 top; Mansell Collection: p.10 left, p.19, p.20; Mary Evans Picture Library: p.7; National Library of Scotland: p.8 bottom right; National Portrait Gallery: p.9; Public Record Office: p.14 top, p.15 top; Royal Collection, St James's Palace © HM The Queen: p.11 top, p.12 left, p.18 bottom; Scotland in Focus: p.11 bottom left, p.13 top, p.15 left and bottom right, p.16 top; Scottish National Portrait Gallery: p.5 top, p.10 right, p.14 bottom; Scottish Records Office: p.5 bottom; Towneley Hall Art Galleries and Museums: p.6 bottom; Victoria and Albert Museum: p.1

Cover photograph reproduced with permission of The Royal Collection, © HM Queen Elizabeth II.

Our thanks to Meg Lorimer of Burgh Primary School, Galashiels for her comments in the preparation of this book.

Every effort has been made to contact copyright holders of any material reproduced in this book. Any omissions will be rectified in subsequent printings if notice is given to the Publisher.

Contents

The young queen

ABOVE:
Linlithgow Palace:
Mary was born
here. When her
father, James V,
was told of her
birth, he said: 'It
cam wi' a lass. It
will gang wi' a
lass.' His family,
the Stewarts, had
become kings
through marriage
to the daughter of
Robert the Bruce.
He thought their
royal line *would*
end with Mary.

RIGHT:
The ruined
Palace of
Linlithgow.

The birth of Mary – future Queen of Scots

Mary was born on 8 December 1542 in Linlithgow Palace. Her father, James V of Scotland, had just been **defeated** by the English at the Battle of Solway Moss. When he was told that the baby was a girl he turned his face to the wall, because he wanted a son. He died a few days later. As Mary's brothers had both died as infants she was the **heir** to the throne.

Marriage proposals

The kings of England and France were both very interested in the news about the new baby. Henry VIII of England wanted England and Scotland to become one kingdom. He suggested that Mary should grow up in the English Court. When she was old enough she would marry Edward, the Prince of Wales.

This was agreed, but Mary stayed in Scotland. Henry VIII attacked Scotland but did not capture the young queen. In 1547 Henry VIII died. In the same year a battle was fought at Pinkie Cleugh, not far from Edinburgh. The English won. It seemed that Mary might be captured. She was taken from Stirling Castle to Dumbarton Castle 60 kms away for safety.

In 1548 the French king, Henry II, suggested that his son Francis, the **Dauphin**, should marry Mary. Mary's mother, Mary of Guise, agreed. In August 1548, the five-year-old Queen of Scots left Dumbarton to live at the French court. Mary of Guise ruled Scotland while she was gone.

LEFT:
Mary of Guise, Mary's mother and the French wife of James V of Scotland.

BELOW:
Mary and her mother wrote many letters to each other. Mary wrote this one in French when she was eleven.

Life in France

RIGHT:
The Dauphin
Francis who loved
and admired
Mary, his
childhood friend.
He died of an
infection in
December 1560.

Queen of France and Scotland
At the French court Mary learned to speak several languages, to sing, to dance, to **embroider** and to ride. On 24 April 1558, at the age of fifteen, she was married to the **Dauphin** Francis in Paris. The Dauphin was given the title of King of Scotland. Mary became Queen Dauphiness. In England, Elizabeth I was crowned Queen of England in 1559.

RIGHT:
Mary returned to
Scotland where
the **Catholic
religion** she
followed had
been **outlawed**.
The leader of the
new **Protestant
religion**, John
Knox, said that
Mary must
change her
religion. She
would not do so.
This picture
shows Knox
trying to make
Mary change her
mind.

The French king, Henry II, said that Elizabeth I had no right to the English throne because Elizabeth's father, Henry VIII, had divorced his first wife to marry Elizabeth's mother. Many people claimed that Elizabeth was **illegitimate**. He said the English throne belonged to Mary Queen of Scots, her cousin. He suggested that Mary should be called Queen of Scotland, England and France when her husband Francis became King of France. Mary agreed with this. Elizabeth I never forgave her.

In July 1559, Henry II of France died after an accident. Francis and Mary became king and queen of both France and Scotland. Mary did not claim to be Queen of England but she did claim to be Elizabeth I's heir.

An eventful year

Events that happened in 1560 changed Mary's life. Her mother, Mary of Guise, died. The Scottish **parliament** signed a **peace treaty** with England. Laws were passed making the **Protestant religion** the **official** religion of Scotland. In December Mary's husband Francis died. No longer Queen of France, Mary decided to return to Scotland – where her religion was not accepted.

ABOVE:
*The French court moved from one **château** to the next. Mary spent part of her childhood at Chambord, a château on the Loire.*

Return to Scotland

ABOVE:
Mary Queen of
Scots dressed in
white, which was
the colour of
mourning in
France.

The welcome

Mary arrived home in Scotland to rain and mist on 19 August 1561. John Knox, the leader of the **Protestant** Church, wrote, 'The mist was so thick and so dark. The sun was not seen to shine two days before nor two days after.' He said it was a bad **omen**. There would be trouble in Scotland. The lack of sunshine and Knox's warning did not stop Mary's **subjects** welcoming her.

She rode into Edinburgh in a grand **procession**. The people of the town performed plays and made speeches to welcome her. Mary did not get much sleep that night. A large crowd gathered below her window in Holyroodhouse, playing until morning on three-stringed fiddles. Mary brought with her wonderful dresses and jewels. All the **lords** and ladies of her court began to wear brightly-coloured clothes, and wigs. The Palace of Holyroodhouse became full of music and dancing.

RIGHT:
The Earl of
Moray, who gave
Mary good
advice on her
return to
Scotland.

FAR RIGHT:
John Knox felt
that women
should not be
allowed to rule
countries. He
thought it was
unnatural.

THE FIRST BLAST
TO AWAKE WOMEN
degenerate.

O promote a woman to beare rule, superióritie, dominion or empire aboue any realme, nation, or citie, is repugnát to nature, cõtumelie to God, a thing moſt contrarious to his reueled will and approued ordináce, and finallie it is the ſubuerſion of good order, of all equitie and iuſtice.

In the probation of this propoſition, I will not be ſo curious, as to gather what foeuer may amplifie, ſet furth, or decore the ſame, but I am purpoſed, euen as I haue ſpoken my conſcience in moſt plaine ãd fewe wordes, ſo to ſtãd content with a ſimple proofe of euerie membre, bringing in for my witneſſe Goddes ordinance in nature, his plaine will reueled in his worde, and the mindes of ſuch as be moſte auncient amongeſt godlie writers.

And firſt, where that I affirme the em-

Left:
This is a portrait painted for the coronation of Elizabeth I of England. Queen Elizabeth suggested that Mary should marry Lord Robert Dudley rather than a Catholic prince. Mary said she would agree if Queen Elizabeth admitted that Mary was heir to the English throne.

Religious differences

Mary travelled all round her kingdom and met many of her subjects. Some were worried that she was a **Catholic** while they were Protestants. Mary took the advice of her half-brother, the Earl of Moray. She made it clear that the people did not have to change their religion. Neither would she. John Knox did not like her because of her religion. He made her life very difficult. He said she should give up her religion. He was worried she might marry a Catholic prince. Indeed, Mary would have to marry again to have a child who would be **heir** to the Scottish throne.

A second husband

RIGHT:

Henry Stewart, Lord Darnley, was very vain. He liked expensive clothes. His **doublet** *has been padded out to give him a fashionable shape. Over his shoulders he wears a French* **cape**.

Darnley

Many princes, **lords** and nobles wanted to marry Mary. In the end she made up her own mind. She met her cousin Henry Stewart, Lord Darnley. He was tall and good looking. Mary immediately fell in love with him. They were married on Sunday 29 July 1565 in Holyroodhouse, early in the morning.

RIGHT:

Mary was very beautiful at this time in her life. She often wore black dresses with white lace collars.

Mary gave Darnley the title of King of Scotland. At first all went well. In Holyroodhouse they held **banquets** attended by several hundred people. They dressed up as gods and goddesses. They sang, danced and played musical instruments. At Falkland Palace they played tennis or hunted stags and wild pigs. At St Andrews they took part in archery contests, or played chess or **billiards.**

Mary seemed to have made a good decision by marrying Darnley. He, like Mary herself, had a claim to the English throne.

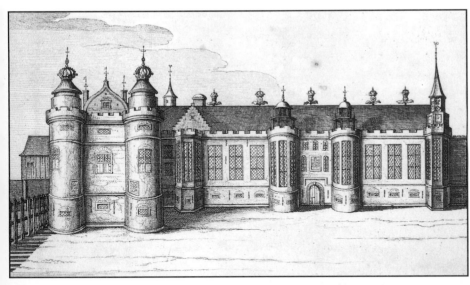

LEFT:
The royal Palace of Holyroodhouse — the scene of many sad and happy occasions.

BELOW LEFT:
Craigmillar Castle was one of the castles where Mary Queen of Scots stayed several times.

Moray's rebellion

Up until her marriage to Darnley, Mary had received advice and help from her half brother, James Stewart, Earl of Moray. He did not like Darnley. He and some other Scottish lords started a **rebellion.** The armies of the two sides followed each other around the countryside. They never actually met to fight in what was called the Chaseabout Rebellion. Moray and the rebels escaped to England.

BELOW:
David Rizzio came to Scotland in 1561. He was a good musician and he could talk about many interesting things. Mary liked him and made him her secretary in 1564.

Mary now expected Darnley to help her rule. Although he looked like a king, he was very foolish. He made many enemies and was not able to give any good advice. Mary had to find someone whose advice she could trust. She chose David Rizzio, her Italian **secretary.**

A ruined marriage

RIGHT:
The scene of Rizzio's murder – Queen Mary's room in Holyroodhouse.

It soon became clear that Mary had made a mistake by marrying Darnley. He began acting like a spoilt child. When Mary became pregnant in 1565 he continued to spend his time hunting and riding. He demanded to be crowned King of Scotland instead of just using the title.

ABOVE:
*The coats of arms of Mary and Francis II of France were painted on the ceiling of Queen Mary's outer **chamber** in Holyroodhouse.*

It became obvious that Darnley had married Mary just to get the throne. Mary told him that only the Scottish **parliament** could make him king. He did not believe her. He became even angrier when David Rizzio, Mary's **secretary,** said it was true.

David Rizzio had become Mary's friend as well as her **adviser.** Left alone by Darnley, Mary began to spend a lot of time with Rizzio. Darnley became more and more jealous of him and decided that he must die. He was not the only one to think so. A group of Scottish nobles, led by James Douglas, Earl of Morton, with Ruthven, Lindsay and Maitland, thought that Rizzio, a **Catholic**, had become too powerful. They also saw him as the enemy of all **Protestants**. They wanted James Stewart, the Earl of Moray, to return to Scotland.

The murder of Rizzio

On 9 March 1566 Morton and 150 men took control of Holyroodhouse. Mary was eating her supper with Rizzio and some friends. Darnley came into her room with Ruthven and the other **plotters.** They pulled Rizzio from where he was hiding behind Mary and stabbed him to death in front of her.

LEFT:
Falkland Palace.
Mary Queen
of Scots spent
some time here
with her son,
James VI.

BELOW:
Mary Queen of
Scots and her
son, James VI.

Darnley's murder

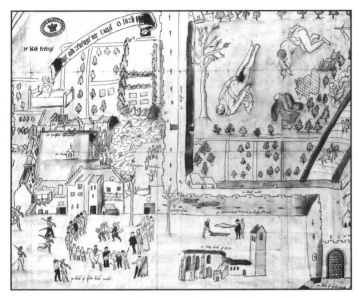

ABOVE:
This drawing shows Darnley and his servant lying in a garden outside the walls of Edinburgh. They may have tried to leave Kirk O'Field before the explosion. No-one knows what really happened.

RIGHT:
The Earl of Bothwell. Mary Queen of Scots married him because she thought the Scottish nobles wanted her to.

Escape from Holyroodhouse

After Rizzio's murder, Mary was kept prisoner in Holyroodhouse. She only thought of the safety of her unborn child. She managed to persuade Darnley that the murderers would kill him as soon as they could, so they made plans to escape.

For the next two days they behaved as if nothing had happened. On 11 March 1566, they secretly left Holyroodhouse. They rode to the safety of Dunbar Castle, over 50 kms away. There loyal Scottish nobles came to help Mary. They were led by the Earl of Bothwell, Mary's strongest supporter. Mary and 8000 men marched towards Edinburgh. The murderers fled.

Kirk O'Field

Mary's son James was born in Edinburgh Castle on 19 June 1566. He was christened on 15 December at Stirling. At the end of December Darnley went to Glasgow. He became ill with smallpox but he slowly recovered. Mary persuaded him to come back to Edinburgh to a house called Kirk O'Field. For the first two days and nights Mary nursed him. On the third night she went to a marriage feast.

At two o'clock in the morning of 10 February 1567, Kirk O'Field was blown sky high. Darnley and his servant were found lying in a nearby garden. They had been strangled.

Many people thought that Mary and Bothwell had planned Darnley's murder. Bothwell was asked many questions by the Scottish **parliament** but he was not accused of the killings.

A third marriage

Bothwell wanted to marry Mary. He persuaded 28 Scottish nobles to agree. He then took Mary away to Dunbar. He kept her prisoner there while he divorced his wife, Lady Jean Gordon. On 15 May 1567 they were married.

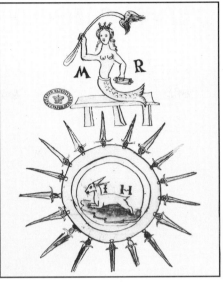

LEFT:
This poster was placed on walls all over Edinburgh. It tried to suggest that Mary (the mermaid) and Bothwell (the hare) took part in Darnley's murder.

The people of Scotland were shocked at this because they thought that Bothwell and Mary had murdered Darnley. Mary and Bothwell had to leave Edinburgh for their own safety. They went to Borthwick Castle.

Some of the Scottish nobles made a plan to make Mary's son, James VI, the ruler of Scotland instead of her. They laid siege to Borthwick Castle. Mary and Bothwell escaped to Dunbar. They gathered an army and marched to Carberry Hill on 15 June 1567. There was no battle, however. Mary's troops deserted her. Bothwell escaped, but Mary was captured and imprisoned in Lochleven Castle. She had to agree to give up being Queen of Scotland.

ABOVE:
Lochleven – a castle on an island. Mary was imprisoned here for a year.

ABOVE LEFT:
Borthwick Castle. Mary escaped from this castle disguised as a man.

The captive queen

ABOVE:
Mary stayed
here at
Dundrennan
Abbey before she
left Scotland for
ever.

FAR RIGHT:
This **casket** may
have contained
letters sent to
Bothwell. The
original letters
may have been
written by
different people.

RIGHT:
A small painting
of Mary Queen
of Scots as she
looked while she
was jailed.

Lochleven Castle

Mary was imprisoned in Lochleven Castle for ten and a half months. The Earl of Moray came and forced her to sign an **agreement.** She was no longer to be queen. Her son James was to become king. The Earl of Moray was to rule Scotland until James was old enough to rule by himself.

On 29 July 1567 the one-year-old James was crowned King of Scotland.

Escape to England

Mary was afraid that she would now be killed. With her **jailors'** help, she managed to escape from Lochleven Castle. Once free, Mary quickly gathered together a large army. On 13 May 1568, at Langside near Glasgow, they were **defeated** by the Earl of Moray's army. Mary rode south to the Solway and escaped across the water to England.

The casket letters

Mary thought that she would be taken at once to see Queen Elizabeth I of England. Instead she was kept a prisoner once more, at first in Carlisle Castle and then in Bolton Castle, in Yorkshire, by the order of Queen Elizabeth I. The Earl of Moray and the Scottish nobles did not want Mary to return to Scotland.

> *I am myself a Queen, the daughter of a King, a stranger, and the true Kinswoman of the Queen of England. I came to England on my cousin's promise of assistance against my enemies and rebel subjects and was at once imprisoned . . .*
>
> *As an absolute Queen, I cannot submit to orders, nor can I submit to the laws of the land without injury to myself, the King my son and all other sovereign princes . . . For myself I do not recognize the laws of England nor do I know or understand them as I have often asserted. I am alone, without counsel, or anyone to speak on my behalf. My papers and notes have been taken from me, so that I am destitute of all aid, taken at a disadvantage.*
>
> REPLY OF MARY TO COMMISSIONERS FOR TRIAL AT FOTHERINGHAY, 11 OCTOBER 1586.

They said they had letters which proved Mary had hated her husband and wanted him killed. These letters had been found in a silver casket which belonged to Bothwell.

When the letters in the casket were examined by a group of English nobles they discovered that they were just copies. The nobles could not be sure who had written the **original** letters as they had not seen them. Mary was found neither guilty nor innocent, but Queen Elizabeth I would not let her go free.

Mary had many difficulties during her long imprisonment. She had only a few clothes. When Queen Elizabeth was asked for help, she sent only some old dresses and pieces of black cloth. Some of the castles in which Mary was kept were cold and draughty. She became ill with **rheumatism**. She was always in pain with her stiff joints. She was also very unhappy because Queen Elizabeth I would not meet her.

ABOVE:
Many people plotted to set Mary free. The last plot led to Mary's trial on 15 October 1586 at Fotheringhay Castle.

The long imprisonment

NEAR RIGHT:
*Elizabeth Talbot, Countess of Shrewsbury – wife of Mary's keeper – was very good at embroidery. She and Mary often sat together sewing pictures on **canvas**.*

FAR RIGHT:
*The Earl of Shrewsbury looked after Mary for fifteen years (1569–84). He treated her well. He allowed her to go to Buxton for treatment for her **rheumatism**.*

RIGHT:
In 1585 Mary was taken back to Tutbury. There she was watched carefully.

RIGHT:
*Some panels **embroidered** by Mary.*

Mary was kept a prisoner in England for eighteen years. Many of the English nobles wanted to set her free. Queen Elizabeth I was afraid of this. She herself was a **Protestant** while Mary was a **Catholic**. Several plots to free Mary were made but Queen Elizabeth I always found out about them in time. Mary was moved from castle to castle and was allowed less and less freedom.

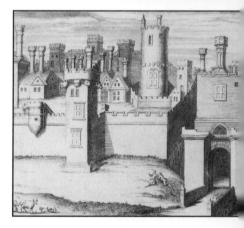

The Babington Plot – 1586

At Christmas of 1585 Mary was taken to Chartley Hall. Here an English **spy**, Sir Francis Walsingham, read all the letters that Mary had smuggled in and out. A wealthy Catholic knight, Sir Anthony Babington, made new plans. He suggested that Queen Elizabeth I should be killed. Mary would then become Queen of England and all the Catholics could worship in the way they wanted. He told Mary that King Philip II of Spain would help them. When Mary wrote letters to Babington agreeing to the plot she was arrested and put on **trial** for **treason.**

Mary was taken to Fotheringhay Castle on 25 September to stand trial. Before it began there were many arguments. Mary was not one of Queen Elizabeth's subjects and could not be tried by English law. She was a queen and could only be judged by another queen. The trial would not be legal. No-one listened.

ABOVE:
*The Earl of Shrewsbury and the Earl of Kent were sent to read Mary the **warrant** for her execution.*

The execution of Mary

Mary was put on **trial** at Fotheringhay Castle on 15 October 1586 because of the Babington plot. Although she said she was innocent, she was found guilty of **treason.**

On Tuesday 7 February 1587 she was told that she would be **executed** the next day. She appeared calm. She wrote some letters. She made a will and she prayed.

At eight o'clock the next morning she was led to the **scaffold.** She placed her head on the block. After three blows of the axe she was dead.

RIGHT:
At eight o'clock Mary climbed the stairs to the scaffold. She crossed herself and sat down on a chair. The warrant of execution was read and prayers were said. Mary took off her veil and dress. Under it she wore a red petticoat. She placed her head on the block. The axe rose and fell three times. The executioner held up her head. Only one man spoke, saying, 'So perish all Queen Elizabeth's enemies.' The others were silent.

MARIA SCOTIÆ REGINA GALL. & DOTARIA REGNORU. ANGLIÆ ET HYBERNIÆ VERÆ PRINCEPS LEGITIMA IACOBI MAGNÆ BRITANIÆ REGIS MATER, A SVIS OPPRESSA ANº DNI 1568 AVXILIA SPE ET OPINIONE A COGNATA ELIZABETHA IN ANGLIA REGNANTE PMISSI EO DESCENDIT, IBIQVE CONTRA IVS GENTIVM ET PROMISSI FIDEM CAPTIVA RETENTA, POSTCAPTI VITATIS ANº 19, RELIGIONIS ERGO, EIVSDEM ELIZ. PERFIDIA ET SENATVS ANGLICI CRVDELITATE, HORRENDA CAPITIS LATA SENTENTIA NECI TRADITVR, AC 12. CAL. MARTII 1587 IN AVDITO EXEMPLO A SERVILI ET ABIECTO CARNIFICE TETRV N MOREM CA PITE TRVNCATA EST, ANNO ÆTATIS REGNIQVE 45

IOANNA KENNETHIE. ELIZABETHA CVRLE.

AVLA FODRINGHAMII.

REGINAM SERENISSⁿᴬ REGVM FILIAM, VXOREM ET MATREM ASTANTIBVS COMMISSARIIS ET MINISTRIS R. ELIZABETHÆ CARVFEN SECVRI PERCVTIT ATQ; VNO ET ALTERO ICTV TRVCVLENTER SAVCIATA TERTIO EI CAPVT ABSCINDIT.

PRIMA QVOAD VIXIT COL. SCOT. PARENS ET FVND.

SIC FVNESTVM ASCENDIT PADVLATVM REGINA QVONDAM GALLIARV ET SCOTIÆ FLOREN 18ᵐⁱ INVICTO SED PIO ANIMO TYRANNIDEM EXPROBRAT ET PERFIDIAM FIDEM CATOLICAM PROFITETVR, ROMANÆ ECCLESIA

LEFT:
The scaffold was put up in the hall in which the trial had taken place. Everything was covered in black. Mary was also dressed in black. She wore a chain round her neck and beads at her waist. She carried an ivory **crucifix**.

Glossary

adviser – a person who gives advice or helps to make decisions

agreement – a strict promise, usually written

banquets – feasts

billiards – a game played on a table which has pockets at each corner, using solid wooden balls and a tapered stick called a cue

canvas – strong cloth used for embroidery

cape – a short cloak

casket – a small box

Catholic religion – a Christian religion which has the Pope in Rome as its leader

chamber – a room in a palace where visitors are met

château – a French castle or large house

crucifix – a cross with the figure of Christ carved on it

Dauphin – the oldest son of the king of France

defeated – beaten or overcome

doublet – a close fitting jacket worn by men during the 15th and 16th centuries

embroider – to make a design or picture on cloth using a needle and thread

executed – put to death

heir – a person who gets the title and belongings of someone who dies

illegitimate – a child born to parents who are not married

jailor – the person who is in charge of prisoners in a jail

lords – men who help a king or queen look after all the land in their kingdom

official – approved of by the government

omen – a sign of what might happen in the future

original – the first one

outlawed – not within the law

parliament – a group of people gathered together to make laws

peace treaty – an agreement made to stop a war

plotters – people who make secret plans

procession – a long line of people marching to celebrate something

Protestant religion – a Christian religion which follows the ideas of Luther who, in 1517, spoke out against the way the church was being run

rebellion – an uprising against a leader

rheumatism – a disease which makes the joints stiffen

royal line – the members of the ruling royal family

scaffold – a raised wooden platform usually used for executions

secretary – a person who writes or makes arrangements for another person

spy – a person who secretly watches others

subject – a person ruled by another

trial – a gathering where someone's guilt or innocence is proved

treason – a crime against the country or the ruler of the country

warrant – a written order

Timeline 1542–1587

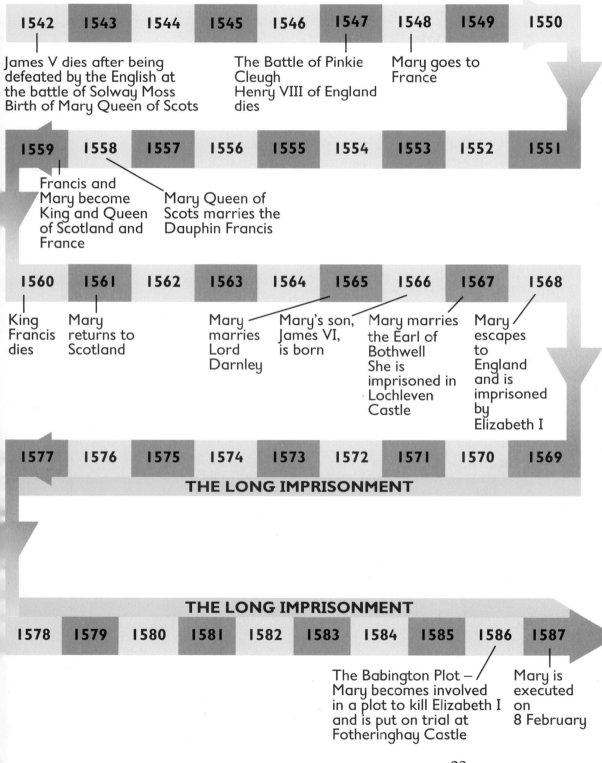

| 1542 | 1543 | 1544 | 1545 | 1546 | 1547 | 1548 | 1549 | 1550 |

James V dies after being defeated by the English at the battle of Solway Moss
Birth of Mary Queen of Scots

The Battle of Pinkie Cleugh
Henry VIII of England dies

Mary goes to France

| 1559 | 1558 | 1557 | 1556 | 1555 | 1554 | 1553 | 1552 | 1551 |

Francis and Mary become King and Queen of Scotland and France

Mary Queen of Scots marries the Dauphin Francis

| 1560 | 1561 | 1562 | 1563 | 1564 | 1565 | 1566 | 1567 | 1568 |

King Francis dies

Mary returns to Scotland

Mary marries Lord Darnley

Mary's son, James VI, is born

Mary marries the Earl of Bothwell
She is imprisoned in Lochleven Castle

Mary escapes to England and is imprisoned by Elizabeth I

| 1577 | 1576 | 1575 | 1574 | 1573 | 1572 | 1571 | 1570 | 1569 |

THE LONG IMPRISONMENT

THE LONG IMPRISONMENT

| 1578 | 1579 | 1580 | 1581 | 1582 | 1583 | 1584 | 1585 | 1586 | 1587 |

The Babington Plot – Mary becomes involved in a plot to kill Elizabeth I and is put on trial at Fotheringhay Castle

Mary is executed on 8 February

Index